OH THE
piZZabiLiTies

ISBN-13: 978-1-56383-596-4
Item #7145

**Printed in the USA
by G&R Publishing Co.**

Distributed By:

507 Industrial Street
Waverly, IA 50677

www.cqbookstore.com

gifts@cqbookstore.com

 CQ Products

 CQ Products

 @cqproducts

 @cqproducts

satisfy your pizza craving!

Need pizza but tired of the same old thing? This book has new spins on your favorite food so you'll never be bored again!

Every recipe makes a delish pizza-ish dish. You'll find hot melty pizza toppings *(from the simple to the deluxe)* piled onto super flavorful traditional crusts and wildly delicious nontraditional ones. Be inspired by mash-ups that combine different ethnic foods – like Italian pizza plus Mexican quesadillas *(called **pizzadillas**)* – and fall in love when you double-down on Italian dishes, like pizza stuffed inside calzones *(**pizzones**)*. To top it all off, there are pizza-like wedges of scrumptious appetizers and desserts, perfect for sharing. Any way you slice it, this is your piece of pizza heaven!

Use these tips for pizzeria-style creations at home.

1 Crusts, sauces, and toppings can be easily interchanged, so experiment! You're sure to find favorite new combos.

2 Homemade sauces are easy to make and add a distinctive flavor to these recipes. Store them in airtight containers in the fridge for up to a week or freeze in 1-cup portions for longer storage.

3 Crust recipes use all-purpose flour *("flour")* unless listed differently. Ramp up the fiber and nutrition in any of these crusts by substituting up to 25% of the AP flour with whole wheat flour.

4 To help dough rise, cover the bowl with a damp towel or plastic wrap to keep it moist, and set it in a warm spot *(like on top of a warm stovetop, on a heating pad, or on the upper rack inside a cold oven with a pan of hot water on the lower rack).*

5 No time for homemade crusts? No problem. There are plenty of yummy ready-to-bake crusts or quick mixes available.

Stuffed Crust Taco **Pizza**

1 (13.8 oz.) tube refrigerated pizza crust

8 (.75 oz.) sticks string cheese *(we used mozzarella & cheddar twists)*

1 lb. ground beef

½ C. taco sauce

2 to 3 T. taco seasoning

1½ C. shredded Mexican cheese blend

½ C. sour cream

Shredded lettuce

1 C. chopped tomato

Sliced black olives

Diced fresh avocado

1 C. broken taco-flavored tortilla chips

Your favorite salsa

Preheat the oven to 425° and grease a 12" pizza pan. Unroll dough and press into the pan, leaving about 1" of dough hanging over the edge. Set string cheese sticks around inside edge of crust and fold dough over cheese, pinching to seal the cheese inside. Prebake the crust for 8 to 10 minutes or until set and lightly browned around edges.

Meanwhile, brown the ground beef in a skillet over medium heat until cooked and crumbly; drain. Stir taco sauce and taco seasoning into the beef. Remove crust from the oven and spread with beef mixture; sprinkle with cheese. Bake 8 to 10 minutes longer, until cheese is melted and crust is done. Spoon sour cream onto pizza and top with lettuce, tomato, olives, avocado, and tortilla chips. Serve with salsa.
Makes 1 (12") pizza

With a cheese-filled crust and all these toppings, this taco pizza is a hearty meal. Oh, and don't forget to dip the stuffed crust into some salsa for even more "Mmmm..."

Serves 6-12

Make 'em ahead of time for an easy pizza-craving fix now or later.

Pizza Sliders

1 (12 ct.) pkg. dinner rolls *(we used King's Hawaiian Sweet)*

Pizza sauce

½ lb. sage-flavored pork sausage, browned & drained

¼ lb. sliced salami *(we used peppered salami)*

½ C. sliced black olives

2 C. shredded mozzarella cheese

¼ C. butter, melted

2 T. grated Parmesan cheese

2 T. chopped fresh parsley

¾ tsp. garlic powder

½ tsp. dried oregano

Black pepper

Preheat the oven to 375°. Line a 7 x 11" baking pan with foil and spritz with cooking spray. Slide the rolls out of their package, slice them horizontally as a unit, and place the bottoms in the lined pan; set aside the tops. Spread a thin layer of pizza sauce over the rolls in pan. Top evenly with the sausage, salami, olives, and cheese. Place the set-aside tops over the fillings.

In a small bowl, whisk together the butter, Parmesan, parsley, garlic powder, oregano, and pepper to taste. Brush half the butter mixture over the dinner rolls. Bake 20 to 25 minutes, until fillings are hot and melty, covering with foil if buns are getting too dark. Brush with the remaining butter mixture and serve promptly.

Junk Pizza

For a great way to use leftovers, top a split Vienna loaf with any sauces, toppings, and cheese accumulating in your fridge. Bake at 375° on the bottom oven rack for 10 minutes, then increase the temperature to 425° and bake in the upper third of the oven 10 minutes more or until heated through. (We used tomato sauce, sun-dried tomato pesto, jarred hot chili peppers, diced tomatoes, bell peppers, cooked meatballs, bacon, onion, Romano and mozzarella cheeses, and black pepper. Oh yum!) **Serves 4**

Use large egg roll wrappers to enclose all this pizza yumminess. What could be tastier?

Pizza Rolls

Cut 3 mozzarella string cheese sticks in half crosswise. Set 1 egg roll wrapper on a flat surface with one bottom corner nearest you, like a diamond. Spread 2 tsp. pizza sauce horizontally across the center, leaving 1" at side corners uncovered. Sprinkle with Italian seasoning and layer on 5 pepperoni slices, chopped mushrooms, and 1 cheese piece. Fold bottom corner of wrapper over the filling and roll a quarter turn; tuck in side corners and roll another quarter turn. Moisten the top corner of wrapper with water and finish rolling into a log, sealing well. Make five more rolls. Deep-fry in 2" of hot vegetable oil *(360° to 375°)* until golden brown, about 2 minutes. Drain on paper towels and sprinkle with garlic salt and grated Parmesan. Dip into pizza sauce.

Serves 4

No crust, just pure pizza-love!

Pizza-Stuffed Chicken Breasts

Preheat the oven to 375°. With a sharp knife, cut a slit in one side of 4 large boneless, skinless chicken breast halves to make a big pocket in each. Stuff pockets with 1 T. pizza sauce *(we used Balsamic Pizza Sauce on page 25)*, 1 slice fresh mozzarella cheese, 3 pepperoni slices, and 1 whole basil leaf. Arrange in a large baking dish and brush with 1 T. olive oil. Sprinkle with 2 tsp. dried oregano and season with salt and black pepper. Bake until chicken is cooked through, 30 to 40 minutes. Garnish with fresh basil and shredded Romano cheese. Serve over cooked pasta, if you'd like.

An easy-to-handle crust with whole wheat flour, loaded with grilled summer veggies, makes this pizza "grillicious" and nutritious.

Grilled Veggie **Pizza**

⅔ C. warm water
(*110° to 115°*)

1 tsp. active dry yeast
(*not instant*)

2 T. olive oil

2¼ C. flour

¼ C. whole wheat flour

1 tsp. salt

1 small zucchini,
sliced & quartered

1 green bell pepper,
diced

1 small yellow squash,
sliced & quartered

1 C. sliced mushrooms

Spicy Garlic Oil
(*recipe on page 11*)

5 to 6 plum tomatoes,
diced

2 C. shredded fontina
cheese

¼ C. grated Parmesan
cheese

Coarse salt and black
pepper

In the bowl of a stand mixer, mix warm water and yeast; let stand 5 minutes to dissolve. Whisk in the oil, then stir in both flours and salt until dough forms. Knead with a dough hook on low speed for 5 to 7 minutes *(or by hand on a floured surface)* until smooth. Cut dough into four even pieces and place in an oiled baking pan, turning once to coat. Cover and let rise in a warm place until doubled, 1 to 1½ hours.

Preheat the grill *(with a grill pan)* to 400°. Toss the zucchini, bell pepper, squash, and mushrooms in a bowl with 2 T. Spicy Garlic Oil. Transfer veggies to the grill pan and cook about 5 minutes, until tender and browned on all sides; set aside. Reduce grill heat and oil the grate. Flatten dough pieces into 9" disks; set on the grate and cook until browned on the bottom, 1 to 2 minutes. Remove crusts and flip over onto a cookie sheet. Brush the browned side with Spicy Garlic Oil and top with the grilled veggies, tomatoes, and both cheeses. Return pizzas to grill, close the lid, and cook over indirect heat until bottoms are browned and cheese is melted, 2 to 4 minutes. Season with salt and pepper to taste before serving.

Spicy Garlic Oil

Mix ⅓ C. olive oil, 4 tsp. minced garlic, and ½ tsp. red pepper flakes in a small saucepan over medium heat and cook until garlic begins to sizzle, 2 to 3 minutes. Transfer to a heat-safe bowl and let cool.

Makes 1 (12") pizza

This hearty appetizer will make everyone happy...promise!

Crabby Pizza

Place a baking stone *(or pizza pan)* in the oven as it preheats to 450°. In a medium bowl, whisk together 1 (8 oz.) pkg. softened cream cheese and 3 T. mayonnaise until smooth and creamy. Add 2 tsp. lemon juice, 2 T. Worcestershire sauce, and ⅛ tsp. each black pepper and garlic salt; stir well. Mix in ¼ C. frozen chopped spinach *(thawed & well-drained)* and 1 sliced green onion. Thoroughly drain 2 (4 oz.) cans crabmeat and remove any cartilage; stir into the cream cheese mixture until well combined. Lightly brush 1 (12") ready-to-use pizza crust with olive oil, then spread crab mixture on top, leaving a 1" border around edge. Sprinkle with ½ C. shredded Italian 4-cheese blend and bake 11 to 15 minutes, until golden brown and bubbly. Let stand a few minutes, then top with sliced grape tomatoes and more green onion before slicing.

Makes 1 (12") pizza

A sweet-and-hot flavor combo smothered with cheesy goodness – simply luscious.

Pineapple-Pulled Pork **Pizza**

Preheat your oven to 500° and place a 12" ready-to-use pizza crust on a pizza pan. Stir together ⅓ C. barbecue sauce and 1 T. pineapple juice and spread over the crust. Top with 1 C. *(about ⅔ lb.)* purchased or homemade barbecued pulled pork, 1 C. fresh pineapple chunks, 6 oz. bacon *(cooked crisp & crumbled)*, 1 jalapeño *(seeded & very thinly sliced)*, and 1½ C. shredded Pepper Jack or Colby Jack cheese. Bake 8 to 12 minutes or until the cheese is melted and everything is hot. Remove from the oven and toss on some fresh cilantro before serving.

Makes 1 (9") pizza

A feel-good, gluten-free pizza crust that's sturdy enough to handle any of your favorite toppings.

Cauliflower Crust Pizza

- 1 medium head cauliflower
- 1 egg
- ½ C. shredded Parmesan cheese
- ½ C. shredded Asiago cheese
- 1 tsp. Italian seasoning
- ½ tsp. garlic powder
- ¼ tsp. red pepper flakes
- ¼ tsp. black pepper
- 1¼ C. cooked, shredded chicken
- ½ C. barbecue sauce
- 1 C. shredded mozzarella and/or Pepper Jack cheese
- ¼ C. thinly sliced red onion
- Fresh cilantro

Preheat the oven to 400° and line a pizza pan with parchment paper. Grate the cauliflower florets until rice-like, and lightly pack to measure 2 C. Place cauliflower in a large, dry nonstick skillet and cook over medium heat 8 to 10 minutes, stirring occasionally, until much of the moisture has evaporated. Set aside to cool.

Meanwhile, whisk the egg in a medium bowl; mix in the Parmesan and Asiago cheeses and all the seasonings. Add the cooled cauliflower and stir well. Place crust mixture on the parchment paper and pat "dough" into a 9" circle about ¼" thick. Prebake 20 minutes, until crust is set and golden brown; let cool several minutes. Combine the chicken and barbecue sauce; spread over crust, all the way to the edges. Top with mozzarella and onion. Return to the oven and bake 10 to 15 minutes more. Carefully transfer the pizza off the paper to a cooling rack and let stand a few minutes before cutting. Garnish with cilantro.

Broccoli Crust

Prepare a broccoli crust the same way as cauliflower crust on previous page, substituting grated fresh broccoli florets. Shorten the first baking time to 15 minutes. Top with shredded Colby Jack cheese, crumbled bacon, sliced tomatoes, diced artichokes, sliced garlic and shallots, and more cheese; bake 10 minutes more. To serve, top with fresh arugula, spinach, basil, and shredded Asiago.
Makes 1 (9") pizza

Lasagna roll-ups are easy and delish – and they're even better when they taste like pizza!

Pizzagna Roll-Ups

10 lasagna noodles

2 C. pizza sauce, divided

6 oz. cream cheese, softened

¾ C. plain Greek yogurt

2 C. shredded Italian 5-cheese blend, divided

2 T. chopped fresh parsley

1 tsp. Italian seasoning

1 tsp. minced garlic

1 tsp. onion powder

1 tsp. salt

2 medium carrots, finely shredded, optional

1 C. chopped mushrooms

20 sandwich-size slices Canadian bacon

Sliced black and/or green olives

Preheat the oven to 350° and lightly grease a 9 x 13" baking dish. Cook noodles in lightly salted boiling water to al dente according to package directions; drain, rinse, and lay flat on two large cookie sheets. Meanwhile, spread 1 C. pizza sauce over the bottom of the prepped dish and mix the cream cheese, yogurt, ½ C. shredded cheese, parsley, and all seasonings until well blended.

Spread cream cheese mixture over the length of each noodle and layer with some carrots (if using), mushrooms, and 2 Canadian bacon slices. Roll up each noodle and arrange in a single layer in dish, seam side down. Spread the remaining 1 C. sauce over the top and sprinkle with the remaining 1½ C. shredded cheese; top with olives. Bake 45 to 50 minutes or until cheese is melted and rolls are heated through. **Serves 5-10**

Serves 8

Party-perfect pizza fun for everyone!

Pizza Pull-Aparts

Press 1 C. finely chopped tomatoes between paper towels to remove excess juice; set aside. Slice a 1 lb. loaf of Italian or Vienna bread in rows 1" apart, cutting through the top without cutting through the bottom crust. Cut similar rows in the opposite direction to make squares or diamonds. Set the loaf on a foil-lined baking sheet. In a small bowl, mix ⅔ C. melted butter and 1 T. minced garlic. Drizzle half the garlic butter and ⅔ C. pizza sauce between the slices. Then fill spaces with ½ C. chopped red onion, the set-aside tomatoes, ½ (5 oz.) pkg. mini pepperoni slices, and 1½ C. shredded mozzarella. Drizzle remaining garlic butter over the bread and sprinkle with Italian seasoning. Cover with foil and bake at 350° for 20 minutes. Uncover and bake 10 minutes more, until bread is crunchy and cheese is melted. Sprinkle with chopped fresh basil before serving.

Makes 10

A crust like no other for bite-size pizza bliss.

Polenta Mini **Pizzas**

Preheat the oven to 450° and line a cookie sheet with lightly greased foil. From a 16 oz. roll of ready-to-use polenta, cut 10 (½"-thick) slices. Arrange on foil and bake 15 to 20 minutes, until firm. Meanwhile, brown ¼ lb. Italian sausage in a skillet until cooked and crumbly; drain and stir in ½ tsp. minced garlic. When crusts are done, spread a thin layer of sour cream over each one and top with some sausage and sliced roasted red bell peppers. Arrange small pieces of fresh mozzarella cheese on top and sprinkle generously with grated sun-dried tomato & basil Parmesan cheese. Increase oven temperature to 500° and bake 6 to 8 minutes more, until bubbly and lightly browned. Remove from oven and top with thinly sliced red onion, sliced grape tomatoes, and chopped fresh basil. Season with sea salt and black pepper and serve immediately.

Serves 4-6

An open-face burrito dressed up like a pizza – the best of both worlds!

Burrito **Pizza**

Olive oil

1 (13.8 oz.) tube refrigerated pizza crust

½ C. chopped onion

½ tsp. minced garlic

1 (15 oz.) can black beans

1 to 2 tsp. ground cumin

1 to 2 tsp. ground coriander

1 to 2 tsp. black pepper

2 C. cooked rice *(any variety)*

1 T. butter

1 (4 oz.) can chopped green chiles

1 C. medium or hot salsa

2 C. shredded Mexican cheese blend, divided

(continued on next page)

1 C. chopped cooked chicken, optional

Salt to taste

2 T. chopped fresh cilantro, divided

1 C. frozen corn, thawed & drained

Sour cream

Preheat the oven to 350°. Brush 1 tsp. oil on a large rimmed baking sheet. Unroll the pizza dough on the pan and flatten into a 9 x 12" rectangle; brush with more oil. Bake for 10 minutes. Meanwhile, in a large skillet, heat 1 T. oil; add onion and garlic and cook until tender, about 5 minutes. Stir in the beans (undrained), cumin, coriander, and pepper; cook for 1 minute. Stir in the rice, butter, and chiles, then remove from heat.

To assemble, spread the salsa evenly over the partially baked crust; sprinkle with ½ C. cheese. Spoon the bean mixture over the cheese, spread the chicken on top, and season with salt. Sprinkle with half the cilantro, all the corn, and the remaining 1½ C. cheese. Bake 20 to 25 minutes more, until crust is golden brown and cheese is melted. Garnish with sour cream and the remaining cilantro and serve hot.

Pizzurrito

Put pizza inside a burrito! Brown 1 lb. ground beef with 1 C. chopped bell pepper and ⅓ C. chopped green onion until cooked and crumbly; drain. Stir in 1 C. pizza sauce, 20 pepperoni slices, ½ C. sliced black olives, and 1 tsp. dried oregano; heat through. Spoon ½ C. beef mixture and ¼ C. shredded mozzarella off-center onto each of 8 warm (10") flour tortillas; fold burrito-style. Brush with melted butter and sprinkle with garlic salt. Grill until toasted on both sides.

21

Makes 1 (12") pizza

Makes two crusts – bake one now, bake one later.

White Mushroom Pizza

In a bowl, combine 2¼ C. bread flour and ½ tsp. each salt and instant/rapid rise dry yeast. Stir in ¾ C. warm water *(110°)* and 3 T. olive oil until dough forms. Knead on a floured surface for 5 minutes; divide into two balls and turn in oiled bowls to coat. Cover and let rise in a warm place for 2 hours. *(Before it rises, you may refrigerate dough overnight or freeze it; set at room temperature for 2 hours before using.)* Preheat the oven *(with a baking stone)* to 525°. Press a dough ball into a 12" circle on parchment paper; let rest. Sauté 3 cloves minced garlic in 2 T. butter for 2 minutes. Stir in 12 oz. sliced mushrooms and 1 tsp. each dried thyme and dried oregano; cook 5 to 6 minutes. Season with salt and black pepper. Brush crust with oil and top with 8 oz. sliced fresh mozzarella, ½ C. ricotta cheese, and the mushrooms. Slide pizza and paper onto the hot stone and bake 10 to 15 minutes.

Makes 1 (14") pizza

Smoked cheese, tender roast beef, and fresh veggies add up to a pretty scrumptious combo.

Smoky Beef Pizza

Preheat the oven to 450°. Heat 1 T. olive oil in a skillet over medium-low heat and add ½ red onion *(sliced)*; cook and stir until soft, about 10 minutes. Sprinkle cornmeal on a 16" piece of parchment paper. Press or roll 1 lb. thawed pizza dough *(we used multigrain)* into a 14" circle on the paper; slide paper and crust onto a 14" pizza pan and press to fit. Spread 1 C. pizza sauce over the crust *(we used No-Cook Pizza Sauce on page 26)*. Layer with the red onion, 1 (16 oz.) pkg. beef roast in au jus *(shredded)*, 2 diced Roma tomatoes, ½ C. shredded mozzarella, and ¾ C. shredded smoked cheddar cheese. Season with salt and black pepper. Bake 15 to 20 minutes or until crust is brown and crisp. Let stand a few minutes before cutting, and sprinkle slices with fresh cilantro and chives.

Makes 3 pies

Pizza plus spaghetti – true love, Italian-style!

Pizzghetti for All

1 lb. ground beef or Italian sausage

1 C. chopped onion

2 tsp. minced garlic

1 red or green bell pepper, chopped

1 (8 oz.) pkg. button mushrooms, sliced

About 2¼ C. pizza sauce or 1 (24 oz.) jar marinara sauce

1 (14 oz.) can diced tomatoes

1 (8 oz.) can tomato sauce

1 tsp. Italian seasoning

½ tsp. each salt and black pepper

1 (16 oz.) pkg. spaghetti noodles, broken into thirds

¾ C. whole milk

2 eggs, beaten

½ C. grated Parmesan cheese

1½ C. shredded cheddar cheese

1½ C. shredded Monterey Jack cheese

1 (5 oz.) pkg. sliced turkey pepperoni

Preheat the oven to 350° and lightly grease 3 (9") pie plates. In a large skillet over medium heat, cook the ground beef, onion, garlic, bell pepper, and mushrooms until beef is browned and crumbly; drain well. Stir in pizza sauce, tomatoes *(with juice)*, tomato sauce, Italian seasoning, salt, and pepper; let simmer, stirring occasionally. Meanwhile, cook the spaghetti to al dente in lightly salted boiling water according to package directions. In a large bowl, mix the milk, eggs, and Parmesan cheese until blended.

Drain the cooked spaghetti and stir into the egg mixture. Divide spaghetti mixture evenly among the prepared pie plates, pressing into the bottom and up the sides of each. Top each with sauce mixture. Cover and bake 40 to 45 minutes, until hot and bubbly. Remove from oven, top with cheddar and Monterey Jack cheeses and pepperoni, then return to the oven to bake uncovered 10 minutes more. Let stand 5 minutes before cutting.

(Unbaked or baked pies may be refrigerated overnight or frozen for up to 3 months. Thaw and bake as directed.)

Balsamic Pizza Sauce

In a food processor, puree 1 (28 oz.) can tomatoes, 1 T. olive oil, 2 tsp. balsamic vinegar, 2 garlic cloves (chopped), 1 tsp. chopped fresh oregano, and salt and black pepper to taste. Simmer in a saucepan over medium heat 15 to 20 minutes or until thickened, stirring occasionally. When cool, stir in 1 T. chopped fresh basil. **Makes about 2¼ cups**

Chicago Deep-Dish **Pizza**

1¾ C. flour

¼ C. cornmeal

½ tsp. salt

1¼ tsp. instant/rapid rise yeast *(not active dry)*

½ C. plus 1½ T. water

3 T. melted butter

1 C. each shredded mozzarella and Monterey Jack cheeses

½ lb. sausage, browned & drained

3 or 4 thinly sliced garlic cloves

1 (14.5 oz.) can diced tomatoes, well drained

1½ tsp. dried oregano

2 T. grated Parmesan cheese

Red pepper flakes

In a food processor, combine flour, cornmeal, salt, and yeast; pulse to blend. Heat water to 120° to 130° and stir in the butter. Gradually add water mixture to processor and pulse until dough forms a ball; process 30 seconds more. Transfer dough to a floured board and knead 2 minutes. Turn dough in an oiled bowl, cover, and let rise in a warm place for 1 hour.

Preheat the oven to 425° and oil a 10" cast iron skillet. Pat the dough over the bottom and up the sides of the skillet. Layer the crust with both shredded cheeses, sausage, garlic, and tomatoes. Sprinkle with oregano, Parmesan, and pepper flakes. Bake 25 to 30 minutes or until crust is done. Let rest a few minutes before slicing. **Makes 1 (10") pizza**

No-Cook Pizza Sauce

Whisk together 1 (6 oz.) can tomato paste, ½ C. water, 1 T. olive oil, ½ tsp. sea salt, ½ tsp. each onion powder, dried basil, and dried oregano, and ¼ tsp. each garlic powder and red pepper flakes until well mixed. Let stand at least 30 minutes before using. Makes about 1¼ cups

A crunchy crust and simple toppings make this pizza an all-around favorite. If you prefer a traditional sauce in place of diced tomatoes, try the **Big Batch Pizza Sauce** on page 37).

Celebrate Italian tradition with this simple, fresh pizza.

Classic Margherita Pizza

In a medium bowl, combine 2 T. olive oil, 3 to 4 chopped Roma tomatoes, 1 tsp. minced garlic, and ½ tsp. salt; set aside at least 15 minutes to marinate. Meanwhile, follow package instructions to prepare 1 (6.5 oz.) pkg. pizza crust mix; let dough rest as directed.

Preheat the oven to 450° and cover a cookie sheet with lightly greased parchment paper. Press dough into a 9 x 12" rectangle on the prepped paper and spread with ¼ C. pizza sauce *(or just brush lightly with oil)*. Top with 6 to 8 oz. sliced fresh mozzarella cheese and the set-aside tomato mixture *(drained)*. Bake 14 to 20 minutes or until lightly browned and bubbly. Remove from oven and top with fresh basil.

Serves 4

Here's a gluten-free, low-carb pizza everyone can pig out on!

Hawaiian Pork Chop **Pizzas**

Trim excess fat from 4 thin boneless pork loin chops and pound between layers of plastic wrap to ¼" thickness. In a large skillet over medium heat, cook 4 bacon strips until crisp; drain on paper towels. Pour off half the bacon grease from skillet. Season chops with salt and brown both sides in the skillet over medium heat. Remove from heat but leave the chops in the pan. Spread a spoonful of sweet barbecue sauce over each chop. Crumble a strip of cooked bacon over each and top with some diced ham, sliced jalapeño or green bell pepper, and a few pineapple tidbits *(drained)*. Set a slice of fresh mozzarella cheese on top and return to medium-low heat. Cover the skillet and cook until cheese is melted and everything is heated through. Sprinkle with fresh cilantro before serving.

This homemade pretzel crust – crunchy outside, tender inside – will make any pizza toppings taste awesome!

Pizza on a Pretzel

1⅓ C. warm water *(110°)*

1 (.25 oz.) pkg. active dry yeast *(not instant)*

2 T. plus ¼ C. honey, divided

1 tsp. salt

3½ C. flour

⅔ C. water

1½ tsp. baking soda

Coarse sea salt

¼ C. yellow mustard

¼ C. Dijon mustard

½ tsp. cayenne pepper

Coarse black pepper

2 T. butter, melted

2 C. shredded mozzarella cheese

1 sweet onion, chopped

1 (14 oz.) pkg. kielbasa sausage, sliced

1 (8 oz.) can sauerkraut, well drained

In the bowl of a stand mixer, stir together warm water, yeast, and 2 T. honey; let stand 10 minutes, until foamy. Add salt and slowly beat in flour with a dough hook until sticky dough forms. Beat 5 minutes more (or knead by hand on a floured surface) until smooth and tacky. Dust dough with flour and lightly shape into a ball; cover and let rest 10 minutes.

Preheat the oven to 425° and line two cookie sheets with parchment paper. Divide dough into six equal portions and flatten or roll out each piece into an 8" circle on the prepped pans. Mix water and baking soda; brush over crusts and sprinkle with sea salt *(discard excess soda water)*. Prebake the crusts for 10 minutes. Meanwhile, stir together both mustards, the remaining ¼ C. honey, cayenne pepper, and black pepper to taste. Remove crusts from the oven and brush edges with melted butter; spread the mustard sauce over crusts *(you may not use it all)*. Top with mozzarella, onion, kielbasa, and sauerkraut and bake 10 to 15 minutes longer, until crusts are golden and cheese is melted.

Cheddar Love

What else tastes great with pretzels? Cheese sauce, of course! To change the toppings on this pretzel crust, divide 1 C. cheddar cheese sauce among the prebaked crusts, spreading evenly. Top with shredded cheddar, pepperoni or shredded roast beef, Parmesan, and dried oregano. Finish baking as directed.

Makes 8

Pizza in a potato – so easy and so satisfying as a meal or appetizer.

Potato Skin Pizzas

Preheat the oven to 400°. Scrub and poke 4 medium-large russet potatoes and rub olive oil all over the skins. Sprinkle with coarse salt and set on a foil-lined baking sheet. Bake 1 hour or until tender; let cool. Slice each potato in half lengthwise and scoop out the insides, leaving a shell ¼" to ½" thick. *(You can use the insides to make the delicious Potato Crust Pizza on page 42.)*

Spoon 1 to 2 T. marinara sauce into each potato shell and fill with 2 to 3 T. shredded mozzarella cheese plus whatever toppings you like *(we used diced ham and red bell pepper, sliced mushrooms, and shredded Italian 5-cheese blend).* Sprinkle with grated Parmesan and black pepper. Return to the oven and bake 5 to 8 minutes more. Pop under the broiler for 1 to 2 minutes for extra browning and crisping. Serve hot.

Makes 1 (14") pizza

This flavor combo may just become your new favorite!

Chicken & Spinach Alfredo Pizza

Preheat the oven to 425° and lightly grease a 14" pizza pan. Place 1 lb. pizza dough *(thawed, if frozen)* on the pan and let stand at room temperature for 20 to 30 minutes, until pliable. Meanwhile, heat 1 C. prepared Alfredo sauce in a saucepan over medium-low heat; stir in 1 (10 oz.) pkg. frozen chopped spinach *(thawed & drained)* and 1 tsp. red pepper flakes. Cook until heated through. Press the dough into the prepped pan to make a rimmed crust and spread spinach mixture over the crust. Top with 1 C. shredded mozzarella cheese, 1 C. chopped cooked chicken, ½ C. crumbled blue cheese, and ⅓ C. cooked, crumbled bacon *(about 4 strips)*. Bake 15 to 20 minutes or until crust is golden brown and cheese is melted.

Why heat up the oven when you can make yummy stuffed personal pizzas on a waffle iron?

Stuffed Waffle **Pizzas**

¾ C. warm water *(110°)*

1½ tsp. active dry yeast *(not instant)*

1 tsp. sugar

1¾ C. flour, plus more for kneading

2 T. olive oil

1 T. dried basil

2 tsp. garlic powder

1 tsp. salt

1 tsp. black pepper

1 C. pizza sauce *(we used Fire-Roasted Pizza Sauce, page 35)*

Diced pepperoni

Sliced green onion

8 slices fresh mozzarella cheese

½ C. grated Parmesan cheese

In a medium bowl, combine warm water, yeast, and sugar; stir and let stand 10 minutes, until foamy. Stir in 1¾ C. flour. Mix in the oil, basil, garlic powder, salt, and pepper until a sticky ball forms. Knead dough on a floured surface for 5 minutes, until smooth; cover and let rise in a warm place for 25 minutes.

Cut dough into eight even pieces. For each waffle, flatten and stretch two dough pieces into 5" circles. Spread 2 T. pizza sauce around the center of one piece, leaving ½" border uncovered. Add some pepperoni and green onion, 2 mozzarella slices, and some Parmesan. Set the second dough circle on top and pinch edges together. Preheat a waffle iron to high and lightly grease. One at a time, place a dough pocket in the waffle iron, close, and cook 3 to 4 minutes or until golden brown, pressing down lightly on handle occasionally. Serve with the remaining sauce.

Short on time? *Use Grands refrigerated Flaky Layers Buttermilk Biscuits in place of homemade dough. Just cut a pocket in the side of each biscuit and stuff with your topping ingredients; seal the edges and cook as directed.*

Fire-Roasted Pizza Sauce

In a food processor, combine 1 (15 oz.) can fire-roasted diced tomatoes, 2 tsp. dried oregano, 1 tsp. each salt and black pepper, and ½ tsp. pizza seasoning; pulse until smooth. Makes about 1⅔ cups

A pizza-style quesadilla – the perfect quick-fix snack or supper.

Personal Pizzadilla

¼ C. pizza sauce, divided

2 (6") corn tortillas, divided

2 tsp. olive oil

1 C. shredded mozzarella cheese, divided

Pepperoni and Canadian bacon slices

Shredded Parmesan cheese

Chopped fresh basil

Preheat the broiler. Spread 2 T. pizza sauce over one side of a tortilla. Heat the oil in a 10" broiler-safe skillet over medium heat. When hot, carefully place set-aside tortilla in the skillet, sauce side up, and sprinkle with ½ C. mozzarella. Set remaining tortilla on top and cook about 1 minute, until cheese in the middle melts. Press down lightly with a spatula, then flip the quesadilla over. Spread remaining 2 T. sauce on top and add the remaining ½ C. mozzarella, pepperoni, and Canadian bacon. Set skillet under the broiler for 1 to 2 minutes, just until hot, melty, and beginning to brown. Sprinkle with Parmesan and basil before slicing.
Serves 1

Big Batch Pizza Sauce

Heat 6 T. olive oil in a large pot and sauté 3 C. chopped onion and 1½ chopped green bell pepper until tender; add 2 tsp. minced garlic and sauté 1 minute. Stir in ½ tsp. black pepper, 2½ lbs. chopped tomatoes, 2½ tsp. salt, 1 T. sugar, and 1½ tsp. each dried oregano, dried basil, and dried thyme. Bring to a boil, then stir in 1 (12 oz.) can tomato paste and ½ C. beef stock or bouillon. Reduce heat and simmer for 1 hour; let cool. Freeze in freezer bags.

Serves 8

Who says pizza must have a crust?

Pizza Pasta Salad

8 oz. pasta *(we used penne)*

½ C. diced green bell pepper

½ C. diced red bell pepper

1½ C. halved grape tomatoes

1 C. diced mozzarella cheese

½ C. chopped red onion

½ C. sliced black olives

1 (5 oz.) pkg. mini pepperoni

1 tsp. each garlic salt, onion powder, dried parsley, and sugar

(continued on next page)

2 tsp. dried oregano

½ tsp. each dried basil and black pepper

A pinch each dried thyme, celery salt, and red pepper flakes

¼ C. white vinegar

⅔ C. canola oil

2 T. water

¼ tsp. sea salt

¼ C. shredded Parmesan cheese

2 T. chopped fresh basil

Croutons *(we used Pizza Croutons, recipe to the right)*

Follow package directions to cook the pasta in lightly salted boiling water to al dente. Rinse with cold water and dump into a big bowl. Add the peppers, tomatoes, mozzarella, red onion, olives, and pepperoni.

Meanwhile, in a lidded pint jar, combine the garlic salt, onion powder, parsley, sugar, oregano, dried basil, pepper, thyme, celery salt, pepper flakes, and vinegar; cover and shake. Let stand 5 minutes. Add the oil and water and shake vigorously.

Drizzle the dressing over the pasta mixture and toss until everything is coated. Chill about 1 hour. Stir in the sea salt and top with Parmesan, fresh basil, and croutons before serving.

Pizza Croutons

Toss 3 C. cubed day-old sourdough bread with 3 T. olive oil, 1 tsp. each pizza seasoning and Italian seasoning, ¼ C. grated Parmesan cheese, and salt and black pepper to taste. Spread in a 10 x 15" sheet pan and bake at 400° for 5 minutes; toss and bake 5 minutes more, until crunchy. Serve on salads for pizza-liciousness.
Makes 3 cups

Serves 4

Skim off some calories when pizza floats in these boats.

Zucchini **Pizza** Boats

Preheat the oven to 400° and line a 9 x 13" baking dish with foil. In a skillet over medium heat, cook 8 bacon strips *(chopped)* and ¼ C. chopped onion until done; drain and set aside. Cut 2 medium zucchinis in half lengthwise and pat dry. Scoop out some of the pulp with a spoon, leaving ½"-thick shells. Set zucchini shells in the prepped dish. Dice about ¾ of the zucchini pulp and toss it into a bowl. Add most of the cooked bacon mixture and ⅔ C. marinara sauce; toss together. Spoon the mixture into the zucchini boats and sprinkle each with ¼ C. shredded Monterey Jack cheese, the remaining bacon pieces, and a sprinkling of shredded Romano cheese. Bake 25 minutes or until filling is melted, bubbly, and browned. Sprinkle with fresh basil, parsley, or oregano and serve warm.

Makes 6

Morning, noon, or night, pizza is just right!

Breakfast **Pizzas**

In a skillet over medium heat, cook 4 bacon strips until crisp. Drain on paper towels and crumble when cool; set aside. In a medium bowl, whisk 4 eggs. Remove most of the bacon grease from the skillet and set over medium heat. When hot, add the eggs to skillet, cooking and stirring until scrambled and set. Remove from heat and season with salt and black pepper. Halve 3 English muffins and toast all halves to your liking; spread with butter or spreadable garden vegetable cream cheese. Layer each half with shredded cheddar cheese, chopped tomato, scrambled eggs, and set-aside crumbled bacon. Top with chopped red onion and more cheese. Serve promptly.

Makes 1 (16") pizza

A surprising twist on comfort food! Use mashed potatoes in this yummy crust, then top with potato chunks and more good stuff.

Potato Crust **Pizza**

3 to 4 medium-large Russet potatoes, peeled & quartered*

1 (.25 oz.) pkg. active dry yeast *(not instant)*

½ tsp. sugar

1 C. warm water *(110°)*

½ C. olive oil, divided, plus more for brushing

1 tsp. garlic salt

3 to 3½ C. flour, divided

Cornmeal

⅓ to ½ C. prepared Alfredo sauce

(continued on next page)

4 oz. fontina cheese,
thinly sliced

2 C. finely chopped
broccoli florets

3 slices prosciutto,
cut into strips

1 C. shredded Asiago
cheese

1 tsp. chopped fresh
rosemary

Red pepper flakes,
optional

Sea salt

Coarse black pepper

*Or use the potato pulp scooped from Potato Skin Pizzas
on page 32. Mash 1 generous cupful of pulp to make the
crust and cut up the remainder for the topping.*

Cook potatoes in lightly salted boiling water until fork
tender; drain and let cool. Mash enough of the potatoes to
measure 1 generous cupful; cube the remaining potatoes
and reserve for the topping. In a small bowl, mix the yeast,
sugar, and warm water and let stand 10 minutes, until
foamy. Add yeast mixture, ¼ C. oil, and garlic salt to the
mashed potatoes. Gradually stir in about 3 C. flour, until
dough comes together. Shape into a ball and knead on
a floured surface for 7 to 8 minutes, until smooth. Place
dough in a lightly oiled bowl, turning once to coat; cover
and let rise in a warm place until doubled, about 1 hour.

Preheat the oven to 450°. Sprinkle a greased 16" pizza
pan with cornmeal. Pat dough into the prepped pan;
brush with oil and Alfredo sauce. Arrange fontina cheese
over the crust and scatter the reserved potato pieces and
broccoli on top. Layer with prosciutto, Asiago cheese,
rosemary, and pepper flakes, if using. Season with salt
and pepper to taste and drizzle remaining ¼ C. oil over
everything. Bake 20 to 23 minutes, until crust is golden
brown. Cool 10 minutes before slicing.

Savory and delicious. And oh so pretty!

Pizza Monkey Bread

Preheat the oven to 350° and generously grease a
10" Bundt pan. In a large bowl, combine ½ lb. browned,
drained sausage or ground beef, ⅓ C. olive oil, 2 C. shredded
mozzarella cheese, 1 C. shredded Parmesan cheese,
2 T. dried parsley flakes, and 1 tsp. minced garlic. Remove
the dough from 2 (11 oz.) tubes of refrigerated breadsticks
and cut each breadstick into small pieces. Add the pieces
to the bowl and toss everything together until well coated.
Transfer to the prepared pan and bake about 35 minutes or
until browned on top and cooked through. Serve promptly
from the pan or flip out onto a platter; slice or simply pull off
pieces of this cheesy goodness. Serve with warm pizza sauce
for dipping.

Makes 1 (8"-9") Pizza

It's a real pizza crust that's vegan and gluten-free.

Quinoa Crust Pizza

Place ¾ C. uncooked quinoa in a small bowl, cover with water, and let soak at least 8 hours.

Preheat the oven to 425°. Line the bottom of an 8" or 9" round cake pan with greased parchment paper. Drain the quinoa and rinse well with water. In a food processor, combine quinoa, ¼ C. water, 1 tsp. baking powder, and ½ tsp. salt; process 2 minutes, until a batter forms. Pour into the prepped pan and prebake 15 minutes. Flip the crust onto a parchment paper-lined baking sheet and bake 5 to 10 minutes more, until golden brown and crisp around edges. Add your favorite toppings and bake another 10 minutes. *(For this Mexican salad pizza, use enchilada sauce, corn kernels, and black olives; bake as directed. After baking, mash an avocado with 1 T. lime juice and spread over the pizza; top with salad greens and diced tomato.)*

Pizza-topped nachos – with a rich garlic cream sauce, they're perfect for an appetizer, snack, or simple meal. Delicioso!

Pizzachos

1½ T. butter

1½ tsp. olive oil

1½ tsp. minced garlic

½ C. heavy cream

¼ C. milk *(2%)*

Pinch each of red pepper flakes, salt, and black pepper

⅓ C. grated Parmesan cheese

¾ (13 oz.) pkg. tortilla chips

¼ C. diced onion

½ C. chopped salami or Canadian bacon

Other toppings: sliced black olives, green bell peppers, and/or mushrooms

1½ C. shredded Colby Jack cheese

Pizza sauce, optional

In a small saucepan over medium heat, combine the butter and oil. When hot, stir in the garlic and then add the cream and milk. Cook and stir until mixture comes to a boil. Add the seasonings and Parmesan cheese, stirring until thickened. Remove from heat and set aside.

Preheat the oven to 400°. Layer the chips in a large rimmed baking sheet and drizzle with the set-aside sauce. Top with onion, salami, and other toppings of your choice. Sprinkle evenly with Colby Jack and bake about 7 minutes, until cheese is melted and everything is hot. If you'd like, drizzle with pizza sauce or serve it on the side. **Serves 6-8**

Makes 4 (6") pizzas

The flavors of India top this flatbread pizza for an unforgettable pizza experience.

Chicken Masala **Pizza**

1 T. butter

10 oz. boneless, skinless chicken breast, cut into bite-size pieces

2 garlic cloves, minced

2 T. chopped fresh gingerroot

½ C. tomato sauce

¼ C. plain yogurt

2 T. heavy cream

1 T. garam masala

1 tsp. turmeric

½ tsp. smoked paprika

Pinch each of cinnamon, salt, and black pepper

(continued on next page)

48

Squeeze of lemon juice
4 (6") round flatbreads
Olive oil
1 C. shredded mozzarella cheese
Yellow cherry tomatoes, halved
Cilantro and sliced green onion

Melt the butter in a medium skillet; add chicken and cook until nearly done. Stir in the garlic and gingerroot and cook until chicken is no longer pink; set aside.

Meanwhile, in a small saucepan, combine the tomato sauce, yogurt, cream, garam masala, turmeric, paprika, cinnamon, salt, and pepper. Cook several minutes, then stir in the lemon juice.

Preheat the oven to 450°. Set flatbreads on a baking sheet and brush lightly with oil. Spread the sauce mixture over flatbreads and sprinkle with half the mozzarella. Arrange the chicken and tomatoes over the cheese, then top with the remaining ½ C. cheese. Reduce the oven temperature to 425° and bake the pizzas for 10 to 13 minutes, until cheese melts and crust is golden brown. Garnish with cilantro and green onion.

Apple-Bacon Flatbread

Prebake one thin flatbread pizza crust on a baking sheet as directed on the package. Layer the warm crust with ¾ C. shredded white cheddar cheese, ⅓ C. cooked, crumbled bacon (about 4 slices), 2 sliced green onions, and 1 peeled, thinly sliced Ambrosia apple. Drizzle with 1 T. pure maple syrup and sprinkle with cinnamon and more cheese. Bake at 400° for 10 to 12 minutes.
Serves 5

49

Serves 4

Turn spaghetti squash into a delicious gluten-free "pasta" pizza.

Spaghetti Squash Pizzas

Preheat the oven to 400° and line a rimmed baking sheet with greased foil. Cut 2 small spaghetti squash in half lengthwise, scoop out the seeds, and brush the insides with olive oil; sprinkle generously with salt and black pepper. Set cut sides down on the prepped pan and bake 30 to 35 minutes or until tender; let cool about 5 minutes. With a fork, shred the inside of each squash until spaghetti-like. Add ½ C. pizza sauce, ½ tsp. pizza seasoning, and ¼ C. shredded Italian 5-cheese cheese blend to each one; toss together to coat the squash shreds. Layer with your favorite toppings and more cheese *(we used cooked Italian sausage, tomatoes, green and orange bell peppers, onion, and fresh rosemary and oregano)*. Broil 4 to 6 minutes, until cheese is melted and lightly browned.

Serves 12

Love cheeseburgers? Love this fun pizza!

Cheeseburger Bubble Pizza

Preheat the oven to 375° and grease a 9 x 13" baking dish.
Brown 1 lb. lean ground beef in a skillet until cooked and
crumbly; drain and set aside. Open 2 (7.5 oz.) tubes buttermilk
biscuits and cut each biscuit into eight pieces; place in a bowl.
Add 1½ C. pizza sauce and 1 C. shredded Italian 5-cheese
blend and stir gently to coat. Spread biscuit mixture in the
prepped dish and top with the set-aside ground beef,
⅓ C. chopped onion, ½ C. sliced dill pickles, and ¼ C. bacon
bits. Quarter 5 American cheese slices and arrange on top.
Bake 20 to 30 minutes or until golden brown, bubbly, and
no longer doughy. Meanwhile, mix ¼ C. mayonnaise and
2 T. yellow mustard; reserve for serving. Let pizza stand
5 to 10 minutes before slicing. Serve with lettuce, tomatoes,
more pickles, and the reserved mustard sauce.

If you like a thick crust that lets full-flavor toppings shine, this pizza is for you.

Sicilian-Style **Pizza**

Olive oil

2 C. chopped onion

1 tsp. dried oregano

½ tsp. red pepper flakes

1 to 2 T. anchovy paste

1 (28 oz.) can crushed tomatoes

Sea salt to taste

¾ C. Italian bread crumbs

⅓ C. shredded Romano cheese

2 (11 oz.) tubes refrigerated breadsticks

1 C. grated Parmesan cheese

2 C. shredded mozzarella cheese

Fresh oregano and basil

Italian Dipping Oil *(recipe on page 53)*

Heat ¼ C. oil in a large deep skillet over medium heat until shimmering. Stir in onion and sauté about 15 minutes. Stir in oregano, pepper flakes, and anchovy paste until combined; cook 5 minutes. Add the tomatoes and simmer for 30 minutes or until thickened, stirring occasionally. Season with salt and set aside. Meanwhile, in a bowl, stir together bread crumbs, Romano cheese, and 1½ T. oil; set aside.

Preheat the oven to 450° and brush 1 T. oil all over the bottom and sides of a 10 x 15 x 1" sheet pan. Unroll dough and press into prepared pan, pinching seams together and forming a rim. Prebake the crust for 8 minutes, until just beginning to brown. Remove from oven and sprinkle Parmesan and mozzarella cheeses on the warm crust. Spoon sauce over the top and sprinkle with the set-aside bread crumbs. Bake 8 to 12 minutes more, until crust is brown and sauce is bubbly. Let rest 10 minutes before slicing; sprinkle with fresh herbs and drizzle with a little Italian Dipping Oil.

Italian Dipping Oil

In a shaker bottle, combine ½ C. olive oil, ¾ tsp. each dried basil, dried parsley, and minced garlic, ¼ tsp. each dried thyme, dried oregano, and black pepper, and ⅛ tsp. each salt, red pepper flakes, dried crushed rosemary, and lemon juice; shake well. **Makes ½ cup**

Try a pizza-inspired version of french fries. They're fry-zzas!

Pizza Fries

Preheat the oven to 400° and line a rimmed baking sheet with oiled foil. Grind 1 tsp. fennel seed; add to a bowl with 1 tsp. paprika, ¼ tsp. sugar, and ½ tsp. each dried basil, dried oregano, garlic powder, and salt. Stir in 2 T. tomato paste and 1½ T. vegetable oil. Slice 2 large Russet potatoes into thin fries and dump into a large zippered plastic bag. Add tomato mixture, close bag, and work with your hands to coat the fries. Spread on the prepped pan and bake 20 to 25 minutes. Flip and sprinkle with Parmesan cheese and shredded mozzarella; bake 10 to 15 minutes more, until done. Dip into pizza sauce.

Shortcut Fry-zzas: Use 1 (24 oz.) pkg. frozen french fries *(thawed)* and replace the tomato paste and seasonings with No-Cook Pizza Sauce *(recipe on page 26)*. Bake at 425° for 10 minutes, flip, and add cheeses; bake 10 minutes more.

Makes 1 (12") pizza

This 2-ingredient crust holds a load of delicous Greek toppings.

Greek Pie

Preheat the oven to 350° and line a 12" pizza pan with parchment paper. In a medium bowl, stir together 1¼ C. self-rising flour and 1 C. plain nonfat Greek yogurt until dough forms. Turn out onto a floured surface and knead until soft, smooth, and pliable, 5 to 8 minutes. Press dough into the prepped pan. In a small bowl, whisk together 3 T. olive oil, 1 T. dried oregano, 1 tsp. salt, and ¼ tsp. garlic powder; brush over the crust. Layer with any of the following: chopped roasted garlic, sun-dried tomatoes, sliced green or Kalamata olives, marinated artichoke hearts, thin asparagus pieces, diced roasted eggplant, and sliced red onion. Sprinkle with 1 C. shredded mozzarella and ⅓ C. crumbled feta cheese. Bake 25 to 30 minutes, until the crust is golden brown.

Shrimp on pizza? Why of course! It's shrimply marvelous.

Shrimp Slices

1 C. warm water *(110°)*

1 (.25 oz.) packet active dry yeast *(not instant)*

1 tsp. honey

Olive oil

1½ tsp. sea salt, divided

3 C. flour

½ lb. medium peeled, deveined raw shrimp *(thawed, if frozen)*

Cornmeal

½ C. grated Parmesan cheese, divided

½ tsp. coarse black pepper

1 medium zucchini, sliced

1 (11 oz.) can yellow and white sweet corn, drained

1 C. grape tomatoes, halved

Red pepper flakes

½ C. shredded mozzarella cheese

½ C. Italian 5-cheese blend

Chopped fresh basil and/or parsley

In the bowl of a stand mixer, stir together warm water, yeast, and honey; let stand 10 minutes, until foamy. Stir in 1 T. oil and 1 tsp. salt, then slowly beat in the flour with a dough hook until dough forms. Beat 4 to 5 minutes more, until smooth. Cover dough and let rise in a warm place about 1 hour, until doubled.

Meanwhile, preheat the oven to 500°. Heat 1 tsp. oil in a large skillet over medium heat; add shrimp and cook 1 minute, until beginning to turn pink; remove from heat.

Grease a 16" pizza pan, sprinkle with cornmeal, and pat dough into the pan. Prebake the crust for 5 minutes; remove from oven and brush with 1 T. oil. Sprinkle with ¼ C. Parmesan cheese, pepper, and remaining ½ tsp. salt. Layer with zucchini, prepped shrimp, corn, tomatoes, pepper flakes, mozzarella and Italian cheeses, and the remaining ¼ C. Parmesan. Bake 10 to 15 minutes longer, until crust is starting to brown and cheese is bubbling. Let rest 5 minutes before slicing. Sprinkle with fresh herbs and serve.

Hummus-Kale Pizza

Toss 1 C. chopped kale with 2 tsp. olive oil; set aside. Divide ½ C. hummus among 3 (6" to 7") purchased pizza crusts and spread evenly; top with 1 C. chickpeas (drained), 1 diced avocado, the set-aside kale, ½ C. each shredded smoked provolone and cheddar cheeses, 3 T. grated Parmesan, and salt and black pepper to taste. Bake at 400° for 10 minutes, until cheese melts.
Makes 3 (6"-7") pizzas

Makes 2

Pizza goodness stuffed inside a calzone-style crust – splendiferous!

Big **Pizz**ones

- 2 T. cornmeal
- 1 (11 oz.) tube refrigerated French loaf
- 1 (3.5 oz.) pkg. pepperoni slices, chopped
- 1 (6 oz.) can sliced mushrooms, drained
- 1 C. pizza sauce, plus more for serving *(we used Garlic Pizza Sauce, page 59)*
- ¾ tsp. crushed fennel seed
- ¼ to ½ tsp. red pepper flakes
- 1½ C. shredded mozzarella cheese
- 1 T. melted butter
- ¼ C. grated Parmesan cheese
- ½ tsp. Italian seasoning
- 2 T. shredded Romano or Parmesan cheese

Preheat the oven to 425° and line a large rimmed baking sheet with parchment paper; sprinkle cornmeal on top. On a floured surface, divide the dough in half and set at room temperature 15 to 20 minutes.

Roll each dough piece into an 8" circle; let rest. Meanwhile, combine pepperoni, mushrooms, 1 C. pizza sauce, fennel, and pepper flakes in a bowl and stir together. Cover half of each dough circle with mozzarella cheese, leaving at least ½" around the edges uncovered. Top with pepperoni mixture. Fold the dough over the filling, moisten edges, and press together with a fork to seal filling inside. Set on the prepped pan and brush with butter; sprinkle with Parmesan cheese and Italian seasoning. Bake 18 to 20 minutes or until deep golden brown. Sprinkle with Romano cheese and serve with more pizza sauce.

*To make Mini Pizzones, flatten each biscuit from a 7.5 oz. refrigerated tube into a 4" circle. Add sauce and pizza toppings, fold dough over the filling, and seal edges together. Place in a greased 7 x 11" pan and brush with beaten egg; sprinkle with Italian seasoning, garlic salt, and Parmesan. Bake at 375° for 12 to 15 minutes, until golden brown. **Makes 10***

Garlic Pizza Sauce

*In a saucepan over medium heat, sauté ½ C. diced onion in 1½ tsp. olive oil about 4 minutes. Stir in 2 to 3 tsp. minced garlic and sauté 1 minute more. Add 2 (8 oz.) cans no-salt tomato sauce, ½ tsp. each sugar and garlic powder, 1 tsp. each dried oregano and dried basil, and ½ to 1 tsp. salt. Simmer at least 15 minutes. **Makes 1½ cups***

Easy **Pizzalicious** Snacks

Smoky Lemon Pizza

Press 1 (11 oz.) tube refrigerated thin crust pizza dough into a greased 14" pizza pan. Unwrap a 10 oz. pkg. smoked string cheese, pull apart the cheese in strands, and place evenly over the crust. Very thinly slice 1 small lemon, discard the seeds, and arrange the slices over the cheese. Drizzle pizza with 1½ T. olive oil and sprinkle with smoked sea salt and coarse black pepper to taste. Bake at 450° for 12 to 15 minutes, until golden brown and bubbly. Cut into small squares and serve hot. **Makes 1 (14") pizza**

Layered Pizza Dip

Spread 1 (7.5 oz.) container soft cream cheese *(chive and onion flavor)* in an ungreased 9 x 9" baking dish. Layer with ½ C. pizza sauce, ⅓ C. chopped pepperoni, ½ C. shredded mozzarella, and ½ C. shredded cheddar. Bake at 350° for 20 minutes or until hot and bubbly and the cheese melts. Sprinkle with sliced black olives and green onion before serving with crackers *(we used Italian cheese and herb crackers)*. **Serves 15**

Pizza-Stuffed 'Shrooms

Clean a 16 oz. pkg. of medium mushrooms. Remove and discard the stems and gills. In a skillet over medium heat, combine 2 tsp. olive oil, ½ tsp. minced garlic, and 3 oz. chopped fully cooked sun-dried tomato chicken sausage; cook and stir for 5 minutes. Off the heat, stir in 2 oz. softened cream cheese and ¼ C. grated sun-dried tomato & basil Parmesan cheese. Stuff mushroom caps with filling and top with pizza sauce, shredded mozzarella, dried basil, and black pepper. Bake at 375° on a parchment paper-lined baking sheet for 15 to 20 minutes, until cheese is browned and bubbly. **Serves 6-8**

Veggie Pizza Bites

Unroll 1 (8 oz.) refrigerated crescent dough sheet and cut 24 (2") circles. Press into 24 greased mini muffin cups. Poke holes in the bottoms and bake 6 to 8 minutes. Remove from oven and press down centers to enlarge shells; let cool. Mix 4 oz. softened cream cheese, 1½ T. each mayo and plain yogurt, 1 tsp. dill weed, and ½ tsp. each minced garlic, white vinegar, and sugar; season with salt. Fill shells with cheese mixture *(about 1 tsp. each)* and top with chopped veggies and shredded Colby Jack or Asiago cheese. **Makes 24**

Quick Dessert Pizzas

Pumpkin Streusel Pizza

Prepare 1 (6.5 oz.) pkg. pizza crust mix as directed on package. Spread dough on a greased 12" pizza pan. Mix 2 T. melted butter and 1 tsp. cinnamon; brush over dough and set aside. Combine ½ C. each pumpkin puree and brown sugar, 1 C. flour, and 1 tsp. pumpkin pie spice. Sprinkle clumps of the pumpkin mixture over crust and top with ½ C. chopped pecans. Bake at 450° for 8 to 11 minutes, until lightly browned; cool slightly. Mix 1 C. powdered sugar, 1 T. milk, and 1 tsp. vanilla and drizzle on top. **Makes 1 (12") dessert**

Chocolate-PB Pizza

Line a 9" round baking pan with parchment paper. Press 1 (16.5 oz.) roll refrigerated chocolate chip cookie dough into prepped pan. Bake at 350° for 25 minutes. Cool slightly. Beat together 2 oz. softened cream cheese, ½ C. creamy peanut butter, ¼ C. powdered sugar, ¼ tsp. vanilla, and 1 T. heavy cream until smooth. Lift crust from pan with parchment paper and spread the prepped topping on crust. Cut and then top with warm fudge sauce, chopped peanuts, and mini chocolate chips. **Makes 1 (9") dessert**

Caramel Apple Pizza

Grease a 9" springform pan and press 1 (16.5 oz.) roll of refrigerated sugar cookie dough into pan. Bake at 375° for 15 to 17 minutes, until lightly browned. Cool completely. Core and dice 2 large apples *(we used Granny Smith and Jonagold)*; soak in 1½ C. seltzer water at least 3 minutes. Spread 1 C. homemade or canned cream cheese frosting over crust. Drain apples, pat dry, and scatter over frosting. Sprinkle with ½ C. toasted, chopped pecans and drizzle with caramel sauce. **Makes 1 (9") dessert**

Cinnamon Roll Pizza

Thaw 1 (16 oz.) loaf of frozen sweet bread dough and press into a greased 12" pizza pan; prick several times with a fork and set aside. In a small bowl, combine ½ C. each softened butter, brown sugar, and old-fashioned oats plus 1 T. cinnamon; mix well. Spread thinly over the crust and sprinkle lightly with more brown sugar. Bake at 400° for 15 to 18 minutes or until edges are golden brown. Beat together 2 T. softened butter and 1 oz. softened cream cheese on medium speed. Stir in ⅓ C. powdered sugar and ¼ tsp. vanilla to make a glaze. Warm slightly in the microwave and drizzle over warm pizza. **Makes 1 (12") dessert**

INDEX